MW00814774

Ellen DeGeneres

LGBT ICONS

Chris Colfer

Ellen DeGeneres

Neil Patrick Harris

Tegan and Sara Quin

Ellen Page

Ellen DeGeneres

Rae Simons

LGBT Icons
Ellen DeGeneres

Village Earth Press
Vestal, New York 13850
www.villageearthpress.com

First Printing
9 8 7 6 5 4 3 2 1

Series ISBN: 978-1-62524-152-8
ISBN: 978-1-62524-154-2
ebook ISBN: 978-1-62524-159-7
   Library of Congress Control Number: 2014934555

Author: Simons, Rae.

Table of Contents

Here are some words and phrases you'll need to understand:

"To come out" means to let the world know that you're gay. The opposite would be to "be in the closet," where you keep your identity as a gay person a secret.

"LGBT" refers to lesbian, gay, bisexual, and transgender. It's a term that's used for the gay community because it includes as many groups as possible within one name. Some people think more letters should be added, such as Q for "questioning" or "queer," or U for "unsure."

Airtime is the time during which a television or radio show is broadcast. Sponsors "buy airtime" by paying for commercials that run during a segment of the show.

Evangelical Christians believe that the Bible is literally true and the authority on life. They also believe that a personal relationship with Jesus Christ is necessary to save people from going to hell. Because of their beliefs about hell, they work hard to convince other people to believe the way they do, so that people will go to heaven.

Someone who is degenerate is immoral and corrupt.

Someone who is straight is sexually attracted to people of the opposite sex.

Someone who is tolerant is able to accept others' differences. A tolerant person is open-minded. She doesn't expect everyone to be just like her or agree with her.

A lesbian is a woman who is sexually attracted to other women.

Chapter One

Yep, I'm Gay

Imagine you're sitting in your school auditorium with all your classmates around you. The principal gets up on the stage and says he's asking for people to volunteer for a new project. He asks anyone who is interested to stand up.

You're interested. You know the project is something you want to do. But you're also too embarrassed to get to your feet. What if no one else stands up? What if people think you're stupid for volunteering? Maybe your friends will make fun of you.

All these thoughts are running through your mind as you sit there. But then you see someone get to her feet. Then another person stands up. Then another and another. You heave a sigh of relief. Now it's much easier for you to do what you wanted to do all along: you stand up to be counted with all the others.

Now, however, imagine instead that the principal asked all of you a very personal question—and then told all of you who

Standing up to tell people that you're different is a difficult thing to do, especially in a world where many of us want to blend in with the crowd.

could say "yes" to get to your feet. You know you're one of the people who should answer yes to the principal's question—whatever he asked is true for you—but as you look around the auditorium, you don't see anyone else standing up. There's no way you're going to stand up all alone! You stay where you are, and you keep your secret. When only one or two people eventually get to their feet, you even join your friends when they make fun of those people. You feel a little uncomfortable doing it, but even more, you want to fit in. You don't want anyone to laugh at you, and you don't want to be different from the people you like.

Maybe you wouldn't do this—but the reality is this: most of us don't like to stand out from the group around us. It's a natural human tendency. Long ago, our earliest ancestors learned to survive by sticking together as a group. Thousands of years later, it takes a lot of courage to be one of the first people who speak out, take a stand, and tell the world they're different.

A Courageous Woman

In 1997, Ellen DeGeneres did a brave thing. She stood up and told the world she was different. In fact, she came out as a gay woman on prime-time TV. Forty-six million people were watching.

Ellen had been running on ABC since 1994. In the show, Ellen DeGeneres played a funny, awkward single woman. Up until then, viewers had assumed she was just unlucky in love. Then, in the episode that aired on April 30, Ellen's character sits across from her psychiatrist, who is played by Oprah Winfrey. "It's not like I'm looking for perfection," Ellen says. "I just want to find somebody special, somebody that I click with."

"Has there ever been anyone you felt you clicked with?" Oprah's character asks. "What was his name?"

"Susan," Ellen replies.

Ellen's character then gets the courage to admit her feelings before Susan leaves town. She follows Susan to the airport— and then, just as she makes her announcement, she accidentally leans over an open microphone. The whole waiting area hears her say, "Susan . . . I'm gay."

At the end of the scene, the studio audience roared with laughter. Applause filled the room.

Ellen's worst fears had been laid to rest. "If they found out I was gay," she had confessed on *20/20*, "maybe they wouldn't applaud. Maybe they wouldn't laugh. Maybe they wouldn't like me if they knew I was gay." Ellen's loyal fans loved her even more for her honesty and courage.

But not everyone felt the same. Advertisers like JCPenney and Chrysler decided not to buy airtime during the episode. Wendy's would no longer advertise on *The Ellen Show* at all. Evangelical Christian leader Pat Robertson expressed his disappointment at Ellen's announcement, and another religious leader, Jerry Falwell, called her "Ellen Degenerate." Meanwhile, more sponsors refused to run ads on *The Ellen Show*, and eventually, ABC dropped the show altogether.

The same week that Ellen came out on her show, her face was also on the cover of *Time* magazine with the words, "Yep, I'm Gay." The whole world knew now. She had taken a stand, and everyone's attention was on her. Everyone was talking about her.

It wasn't an easy time for Ellen—but she didn't regret her decision. "I decided this was not going to be something that I was going to live the rest of my life being ashamed of," she told *20/20*.

Changing the World

Coming out in 1997 was a lot harder than it is today. The world has changed a lot since then. Today, many more people, including celebrities like Ellen, have come out as being LGBT. It's a little like standing up in the auditorium when there are already a lot of people standing. Many straight people have changed their opinions of homosexuality as well. And we have Ellen to thank for doing her part. She was one of those first people who were willing to take the risk of being honest about who they were.

It's easier to say something is wrong when you don't know anyone who does that thing. In a survey done in the 1990s, only about one out of every five Americans said they person-ally knew someone who was gay. (Of course, those other four people probably *did* know gays—but the gays they knew were still in the closet.) Being gay seemed like something strange and scary to a lot of people.

When Ellen came out as a lesbian, she made it a lot harder for people to think that being gay was something weird or wrong. Through her television show, millions of people felt as though they knew Ellen. They saw her as someone who was kind and funny. They liked her. When she told them she was gay, most of them *still* liked her, even the people who had thought they didn't like gays. She helped them open up their minds, even if just a little, to other gay people.

Ellen appears on the cover of *Time* magazine after coming out on her television show.

Opinions Change!

A Gallup poll in 1988 found that only 11 percent of Americans thought same-sex marriages should be legal. By 1996, that number had changed to 27 percent, and by 2013, more than half of all Americans favored gay marriage.

In 1973, 7 out of every 10 people surveyed by the National Opinion Research Center thought that homosexual relations were always wrong. By 2010, that number had dropped to 4.

Coming Out

When Ellen came out, she did it for herself. She wanted to be true to who she was. But she also did it for the rest of the world. By standing up to be counted as a gay person, she knew she was making it easier for others to join her.

Coming out is a courageous and honest thing to do. But it's an enormous decision. Before anyone decides to take this big step, the Trevor Project recommends answering five questions.

1. Is it safe?

In some parts of the world, being gay is dangerous. Even in very tolerant countries, admitting to being gay might not be safe within certain groups or families. If your physical safety would be at risk if you came out, then you should wait until your circumstances improve, when you know you have a backup plan and a support system. Your safety is more important than anything else.

Around the World

Different cultures have different viewpoints on homosexuality. According to the Pew Research Center, 80 percent of the people surveyed in Canada believe that homosexuality should be accepted. Meanwhile the majority of Europeans have no problem with homosexual relationships: in Spain, 88 percent of the people surveyed in 2013 thought homosexuality should be accepted; 87 percent of Germans agreed; and in the UK and France, a little more than three-quarters of the population accept homosexual relationships. Latin Americans were not quite as accepting of homosexuality as Europeans, with 61 percent of Mexicans in favor of same-sex relationships, 74 percent of Argentineans, and 68 percent of Chileans—but some of the worst places in the world to be a homosexual are in Africa, where in Ghana and Egypt, only 3 percent of the population accept homosexuality; in Uganda, it's 4 percent, and in Kenya, 8 percent.

2. Do you have a support system?

Before you come out, you need to have a support system in place ahead of time. A support system could be your friends. It could be family or your church group. It's anyone you are certain will stand by you no matter what and love you unconditionally.

3. Do you have a plan?

There is no single perfect way to come out. Most of us aren't like Ellen! We're not going to make a statement on a television

What Is the Trevor Project?

The Trevor Project provides crisis intervention and suicide prevention services to lesbian, gay, bisexual, transgender and questioning (LGBTQ) young people who are 13 to 24. The Trevor Project wants you to know that if you don't have a good support system, you can give their workers a call at 1-800-488-7386, 24/7. You can also text them during certain hours or chat online. To find out more, go to www. thetrevorproject.org.

show or on the cover of a major news magazine. Think about what you want to say ahead of time. Decide where and when and how. Be prepared to handle questions from your family and friends. Not everyone approved of Ellen—and most people who come out will face some degree of disapproval. Be ready to face it!

4. Are you able to imagine—and accept—various outcomes?

Everyone hopes that in the end the people they love will accept them. But that may not happen right away. You may take the people you tell by surprise. They may be disappointed or up-set. Parents especially often have hopes and dreams for their children, and having a gay child may not fit into those dreams.

Coming out can take time. It may be a process, as both sides struggle to accept each other's feelings. By being honest, you're paving the way for a more accepting and educated society, just

Coming out and telling friends and family about your sexuality can be very difficult, and coming out isn't the same for every person.

as Ellen did—but some of the people you care about may never fully accept you. If that's the case, you will still be able to live a full and happy life, even without those people's approval.

5. Can you love yourself no matter what?

This isn't always easy. Accepting yourself as the person you are is one of the bravest things you can do, though.

Ellen DeGeneres said she made the decision to come out so publicly, to the entire world, because she wanted others to know they weren't alone. She did it, she said, for all the teenagers who think about killing themselves when they realize they're gay. And she did it for the young, confused girl she herself had once been. It was her way of saying, "I love you," to that young girl.

LGBT
Historical Timeline

Here's what was happening in the LGBT world in the 1990s, when Ellen came out.

1990: In a study of depression and gay youth, researchers find depression strikes homosexual teenagers four to five times more severely than other non-gay young adults. In the five major U.S. cities that have professionally staffed agencies that monitor anti-lesbian and anti-gay violence— Boston, Chicago, Minneapolis and St. Paul, New York, and San Francisco—reports of anti-gay and anti-lesbian incidents have increased by 172 percent in the past five years.

1993: Teena Brandon is murdered in Nebraska. Brandon was born female, but identified with the male gender. When his friends found out that he was biologically female, they raped him and then shot both him and his girlfriend. The same year, the "Don't Ask, Don't Tell" policy is started in the United States armed forces. This means that the military can no longer "ask" if servicepeople are gay, but those in the armed services are not allowed to "tell" anyone of their sexual orientation or to engage in any homosexual behavior if they want to continue serving.

1998: Matthew Shepard, a gay student, is murdered. His death became a rallying cry for organizations fighting for an end to intolerance of all kinds.

Here are some words and phrases you'll need to understand:

A comedian is an entertainer whose act is designed to make people laugh. Comedians get paid to be funny.

Stand-up comedy is a comic style in which the entertainer stands in front of a live audience and speaks directly to them.

When "comic" is used as an adjective, it means something that's funny; for example, you might make a comic face if you want to make your friends laugh. "Comical" means pretty much the same thing. When "comic" is used as a noun, however, it's referring to a person; it means the same thing as "comedian."

Someone who is impulsive does things without thinking things through ahead of time.

A propensity is a natural inclination to be a certain way.

A mastectomy is the surgical removal of a breast that's sometimes necessary when a woman has breast cancer.

Chapter Two

Growing Up

Ellen DeGeneres started out life being pretty ordinary. She was born in New Orleans, Louisiana, in 1958, and during her childhood, she lived there with her parents and older brother, Vance. Her parents, Betty and Elliott, loved her and did their best for her.

As a kid, Ellen daydreamed about what she might do when she grew up. She loved animals, and one of her heroes was Dian Fossey, who spent years studying gorillas in the mountain forests of Rwanda. Ellen wanted to become someone like Dian Fossey, an expert who studied animals. She also thought she might want to join the Peace Corps, a group of volunteers who travel overseas to help improve the lives of people in need. Even as a child, Ellen wanted to make a difference in the world. She wanted to help.

Ellen does her trademark dance moves with Michelle Obama.
As a child, she never dreamed she would be making the world
laugh alongside the First Lady of the United States!

Being a comedian never occurred to her. Growing up in the 1960s, though, she loved to watch *The Ed Sullivan Show*, *The Dick Van Dyke Show*, and *I Love Lucy*. "When I was a kid," she said years later, "I would always watch stand-up comics really closely. . . . It must have been a subconscious thing because at the time I had no idea that I wanted to be a comic."

Meanwhile, things were often tense in Ellen's family. Finally, her parents decided to end their marriage, and Ellen moved with her mother to Metairie, Louisiana. Ellen was thirteen, and now, for the first time, she discovered that being funny had the power to help other people. "My mother was going through some really hard times," Ellen remembered later, "and I could see when she was really getting down, and I would start to make fun of her dancing. Then she'd start to laugh and I'd make fun of her laughing. And she'd laugh so hard she'd start to cry, and then I'd make fun of that. So I would totally bring her from where I'd seen her start going into depression to all the way out of it."

Ellen had discovered the magic of her talent for comedy. "I was helping [my mother] cope with a broken heart," she told *Teen People* in 2006. "It brought us closer together and made me realize the power of humor."

After a few years, Ellen's mother remarried. Ellen moved with her mother and stepfather to Atlanta, Texas. By this time, her older brother, Vance, had his own band, Dark Ages, which was performing back in New Orleans. Ellen had always looked up to Vance. As she saw the attention and popularity that came with Vance's success, she realized she wanted to experience that excitement too. "Everybody knew who he was," Ellen said.

Ellen has always been close with her mother, Betty. Even in hard times, Ellen and her mom always stuck together.

"That's what motivated me to do something, because I watched him get all this attention and glory."

At Atlanta High School, she played on the tennis team and became popular among her classmates. "Ellen was impulsive in a very warm and charming way," said one of her teachers, Sidney Harris. "She had no trouble making friends quickly, and she had no trouble keeping them. Nor can I recall her ever saying a cross word about anyone. . . . She had a propensity for finding the comical in everything."

But things at home were far from comical. When she was

sixteen, her mother was diagnosed with breast cancer. "Everything was a dirty little secret back then," Ellen said. "The fact that she had a mastectomy was not spoken of. She tried to shield me from it a little bit, but she needed my help with recovery and physical rehabilitation. It bonded us even more."

Ellen's relationship with her mother was stronger than ever—but then something truly terrible happened. While her mother recovered from her life-threatening illness, Ellen's stepfather began to sexually abuse her. Ellen didn't want to tell her mother. She didn't want to tell anyone. Instead, she did her best to handle things on her own. Years later, she told *Allure* magazine that she wants girls to know that they don't have to take the route she took. "It's important for teenage girls out there to hear that there are different ways to say no," she said. "And if it ever happens to them, they should tell someone right away."

Being sexually abused wasn't what made Ellen a lesbian. "People I've confided in about this before say, 'Oh, that's why you're a lesbian,'" Ellen told *Allure*. "But I was a lesbian way before that. My earliest memories are of being a lesbian." That was another secret that Ellen was keeping to herself.

After Ellen graduated from high school, she knew she had to get away from her stepfather. She went back to New Orleans, which she still thought of as home, and she attended the University of New Orleans. After one semester, though, she dropped out. Later, she said, "I started college because everyone else was going. . . . I just remember sitting in there and they were talking about the history of the Greek theatre or something and thinking, 'This is not what I want to know.'"

But she didn't know what to do instead. Years later, in 2009, Ellen spoke about this time in her life in her commencement

Ellen talked to students at Tulane University in 2009 about her life and how she found strength to get through hard times.

address at Tulane University. "When I finished school, I was completely lost," Ellen told the group. "I really had no ambition. I didn't know what I wanted to do. I did everything. . . . I shucked oysters. I was a hostess. I was a bartender. I was a waitress. I painted houses. I sold vacuum cleaners. I had no idea, and I thought I'd just finally settle on some job, and I would make enough money to pay my rent, maybe have basic cable, maybe not. I didn't really have a plan. My point is that by the time I was your age, I really thought I knew who I was. But I had no idea. . . . I had no idea what I wanted to do with my life."

Meanwhile, Ellen was also trying to come to terms with her sexuality. When she was twenty, she came out to her mother. "We were walking along the beach," Ellen remembers, "with our pants rolled up and barefoot—and the water was coming in. I said, 'I'm in love.' And she says, 'That's great.' And I said, 'It's with a woman.'"

Betty DeGeneres remembers that her daughter started to cry then. "Maybe I cried with her," Betty admits. But she wasn't horrified or shocked, she says, only worried.

Coming out to your parents is seldom easy. "She never has understood it," Ellen says, "and I don't think she understands it now. But she loves me and she sees how happy I am." Sometimes that's the most you can ask of the people who love you: that they accept you, even if they don't understand you.

Not everyone in Ellen's family accepted her, though. They still loved her, and she still loved them—but they no longer wanted her in their homes. Ellen couldn't help but be hurt.

She continued to struggle with her sexuality, but finally, she accepted herself as a lesbian. When she was twenty-one, she began a relationship with a young woman named Kathy Perkoff.

For comedians telling jokes on *The Tonight Show*, being invited to talk to host Johnny Carson was a dream come true. If Johnny invited a comedian over to talk after he told his jokes to the audience, it was a sign Johnny thought the comedian was funny and had a future in comedy. Ellen believed in her talent, and she made talking with Johnny on *The Tonight Show* a big goal in her young life.

"They were two very creative people, crazy and young and very much in love," said Kathy's sister, Rachel.

Ellen still hadn't found herself professionally, though. And then, once again, something life shattering happened to change the course of her life: Kathy died in a car accident.

Ellen drove by the accident without knowing it was Kathy. When she found out, everything in her life seemed to fall apart. "I was living in a basement apartment," Ellen told the audience at the Tulane University commencement. "I had no money. I had no heat, no air. I had a mattress on the floor, and the apartment was infested with fleas. And I was soul-searching. I was like, 'Why is she suddenly gone, and there are fleas here? I don't understand. There must be a purpose.'"

Ellen started thinking hard about what she wanted from life—and what she wanted to bring to it. She was searching for answers, but she couldn't find any. "Wouldn't it be so convenient," Ellen asked later, "if we could just pick up the phone and call God and ask these questions?"

Since Ellen couldn't call up God on the telephone, she decided to write a letter instead. She wrote and wrote. When she was done with her letter to God, she read over what she had written. Then, suddenly, she made up her mind: she was going to be a comedian—and one day, she would be the first woman Johnny Carson would invite to be his guest on *The Tonight Show*.

LGBT
Historical Timeline

Here's what was happening in the LGBT world during the years that Ellen was growing up.

1958: The U.S. Supreme Court rules in favor of the rights of a magazine to publish material having to do with LGBT issues. This is the first time the Supreme Court rules on a case that specifically addresses homosexuality.

1961: The Roman Catholic Church officially declares that homosexual men cannot become priests. Meanwhile, in San Francisco, José Sarria becomes the first openly gay candidate to run for office in the United States.

1966: The Mattachine Society holds what it calls a "Sip-In" at New York City's Julius Bar. The action is staged to protest a New York State law that says alcohol cannot be served to homosexuals.

1969: The Stonewall Riots occur in New York City, when the police raid a popular gay bar. The Stonewall Riots are considered the birth of the modern gay rights movement and are remembered with Gay Pride events in the month of June all over the world. The same year, Canada legalizes homosexual behavior; before this, homosexuality in Canada was punishable by up to fourteen years in prison.

1973: The American Psychiatric Association removes homosexuality from its list of psychiatric disorders. Up until then, being gay was considered a mental illness.

1977: Harvey Milk is one of the first openly gay people elected to public office in the United States.

1978: The rainbow flag is developed as a sign for LGBT pride, thanks to Harvey Milk. Later that year, Harvey Milk is assassinated.

1979: The first National March on Washington for Lesbian and Gay Rights is held on October 14, coinciding with the tenth anniversary of the Stonewall Riots.

Here are some words and phrases you'll need to understand:

A comedy club is place where people can go to see comedy performances, including stand-up comedians. It's often a bar, nightclub, or restaurant.

A master of ceremonies has the job of introducing speakers, players, or entertainers.

The Emmy Awards is the highest award given to the television industry. The awards are divided up into categories, such as Primetime, Daytime, and Sports.

A nomination means your name has been chosen for an award or a position. You may not win, but at least you're in the running.

A sitcom is short for "situation comedy." Sitcoms are usually based on situations that might happen in ordinary life. They're often funny, and they usually have happy endings.

A spiritual retreat is a time to get away from ordinary life and focus on a person's inner life.

The Grammy Awards recognize outstanding achievement in the music industry.

The Oscars (also known as the Academy Awards) honor excellence in the film industry.

A person who has compassion is able to feel the pain of others—and then reaches out to do something about it.

Integrity means being honest, but it means more than that as well. It has to do with being whole and undivided.

Chapter Three

Being Herself

The tragedy in Ellen's life gave birth to her determination to build a career making people laugh. She was twenty-three when she started writing comedy material. At first, she was performing only for her friends, but then she expanded to local coffeehouses and comedy clubs. Eventually, in 1981, she earned the role of master of ceremonies at Clyde's Comedy Club in New Orleans. The next year, she submitted a videotape of her stand-up act to a national talent contest held by the cable network Showtime. She won the contest, earning the title of "Funniest Person in America." She began taking her standup act around the country, and she even appeared in several HBO specials. Ellen was in the national spotlight now.

She was working hard to make her dream a reality—but it wasn't easy. "You have to be really, really tough-skinned," Ellen said about her life while she was on tour. "There's lots of traveling, lots of being by yourself, lots of really rude drunk people."

Ellen arrives at the 2000 Emmy Awards. During her time on the show *Ellen*, Ellen had been nominated for a number of Best Actress awards.

When Dreams Come True

In 1986, Ellen's hard work paid off—and the scenario she had predicted became a reality. She became the first female comedian invited to sit on Johnny Carson's couch on *The Tonight Show*. "I had created that experience because I wanted it," Ellen said.

After that, Ellen's success continued to grow. But she was still keeping a secret from the world: no one except her family and close friends knew she was gay. "I started this path of stand-up, and it was successful, and it was great," she said to the crowd at Tulane. "But it was hard because I was trying to please everybody, and I had this secret that I was keeping that I was gay. And I thought that if people found out, they wouldn't like me, they wouldn't laugh at me."

Meanwhile, her acting career started with the 1989 Fox sitcom *Open House*. "In *Open House* I was trying to be this goofy character," Ellen said. "She was so over-the-top and so weird." She then worked on ABC's *Laurie Hill*, before being offered her own sitcom on ABC called *These Friends of Mine*. After the first season, the show, co-starring Jeremy Piven and Joely Fisher, was re-titled *Ellen*. Ellen earned Emmy nominations for Best Actress each year during the show's run from 1994 to 1998.

"I got my own sitcom, and that was very successful, another level of success," she said to the Tulane graduates. "Then I thought, 'What if they find out I'm gay? They'll never watch.' This was a long time ago. This was when we just had white presidents. But, anyway, this was back many years ago. And I finally decided that I was living with so much shame and so much fear that I just couldn't live that way anymore."

Ellen talked about coming out with Oprah Winfrey on her talk show. Though Ellen went through hard times after coming out, soon, her own talk show would make her even more famous.

Making a Big Decision

Ellen spent a lot of time thinking and praying about what she should do. In an interview with Oprah, she said, "I think I've always been a searcher. But right before I decided to come out, I went on a spiritual retreat called 'Changing the Inner Dialogue of Your Subconscious Mind.' I'd never been to anything like it before, and all my friends were taking bets on how long I'd last with no TV, no radio, no phone. But for me that was the beginning of paying attention to all the little things."

Finally, Ellen was ready to take the big step. She was ready to stand up and be counted as the person she really was. "It wasn't to make a political statement," she told the Tulane audience. "It wasn't to do anything other than to free myself up from this heaviness that I was carrying around, and I just wanted to be honest. And I thought, 'What's the worst that can happen? I can lose my career.' I did. I lost my career."

Ellen told Oprah that coming out was a turning point in her life that stripped away everything that wasn't really important in her life. She had to come to terms with the fact that not everyone was going to like her. "The whole world was talking about me," she said. "You know, if you're going to be honest with yourself, you have to admit that you go into show business wanting people to talk about you and wanting everyone to know who you are. But that also means there are going to be a whole bunch of people who don't like you."

Ellen's show won awards, thanks to her talent and courage. But despite that, the network decided to let her go. "The show was cancelled after six years, without even telling me," Ellen said. "I read it in the paper. The phone didn't ring for three

Ellen's voice work in *Finding Nemo* earned her new fans and another level of success with young people and their parents.

years. I had no offers. Nobody wanted to touch me at all. . . . I felt like I was being punished. It was a bad time. I was angry, and I was sad."

But in the midst of all this, Ellen realized she had even more power to truly touch people's lives now than she had before she came out. "I was getting letters from kids that almost committed suicide, but didn't because of what I did," she said. "And I realized that I had a purpose. And it wasn't just about me, and it wasn't about celebrity."

Coming Back

Ellen wasn't going to give up. She kept working—and eventually, the work started to come in again. She got an offer to host a talk show. She was asked to be the voice of the forgetful fish Dory in the Disney/Pixar animated film *Finding Nemo*. "I wrote it completely with [Ellen] in mind," *Nemo* director Andrew Stanton said. Ellen also appeared in thirty-five cities for a comedy tour called "Here and Now," which was taped for HBO and ended up being nominated for two Emmy Awards. She also wrote a pair of books, *My Point . . . And I Do Have One*, published in 1995, and *The Funny Thing Is . . .* , which reached the top of the *New York Times'* best-seller list in 2003. The audio version of the book also earned a Grammy Award nomination for Best Comedy Album in 2005. Between 2001 and 2002, she starred in a CBS sitcom called *The Ellen Show*. She also appeared in films such as *EDTV*, *The Love Letter*, *Goodbye Love*, *Coneheads*, and *Mr. Wrong*.

Then *The Ellen DeGeneres Show* launched in September 2003, and in its first year, it earned a record twelve Daytime

Ellen takes home a Daytime Emmy Award in 2006 for her talk show, *The Ellen DeGeneres Show.*

Emmy nominations and won four awards, including Outstanding Talk Show. In the following two years, it earned eleven more Daytime Emmys.

The show became famous for Ellen's fun-loving dance moves, top-celebrity guests, and Ellen's unique comedy. "I want the show to reach people and to be something positive," Ellen said.

The show opened up other opportunities for Ellen as well. She became a spokesperson for American Express in a global advertising campaign, with print ads created by the famous photographer Annie Leibovitz. Ellen also appeared in a series of funny TV commercials that allowed her to combine her love for dancing, humor, and animals.

Success at Last

Ellen had come a long way from the flea-infested apartment in New Orleans! Awards and opportunities kept rolling in.

In 2005, she hosted the 57th Annual Emmy Awards, just a few weeks after Hurricane Katrina had swept through her hometown of New Orleans. She was intent on keeping the evening positive and upbeat, despite the sad events that weighed heavily on her mind. "This is the second time I've hosted the Emmys after a national tragedy," she told the crowd (she had also hosted the Emmys after 9/11), "and I just want to say that I'm honored, because it's times like this that we really, really need laughter." She finished with a joke: "And be sure to look for me next month when I host the North Korean People's Choice Awards."

In 2007, Ellen became the second woman to ever host the Oscars at the 79th Annual Academy awards. "Ellen DeGeneres was born to host the Academy Awards," said Oscars Producer Laura Ziskin. "There is no more challenging hosting job in show

Ellen arrives at the *American Idol* season finale in 2010. Ellen had enjoyed her time on the show, but she was ready to move on after just a year.

business. It requires someone who can keep the show alive and fresh and moving, as well as someone who is a flat-out great entertainer. Ellen completely fits the bill."

"She just sparkles," said Academy President Sid Ganis. "She is such a pleasure to watch. Her wit cuts to the truth of things, but in a wonderfully warm-spirited way."

In 2008, yet another new opportunity came along: Ellen became the face of CoverGirl cosmetics, signaling the world's new willingness to connect beauty both with being gay and being natural. "Beauty is about being comfortable in your own skin," Ellen said. "It's about knowing and accepting who you are."

Then, after singer Paula Abdul left *American Idol*, Fox Network announced in 2009 that Ellen DeGeneres would be joining the judges' table. "We're all delighted to have Ellen join our ninth season of *American Idol*," said the show's executive producer, Cecile Frot-Coutaz. "Beyond her incredible sense of humor and love of music, she brings with her an immense warmth and compassion."

But that warmth and compassion gave Ellen some problems when it came to being an *Idol* judge. She realized that she wasn't a good fit for the program. "While I love discovering, supporting, and nurturing young talent," she said, "it was hard for me to judge people and sometimes hurt their feelings." Instead, she found another way to help up-and-coming musical talent find an outlet for their talents. In 2010, she announced on her talk show that she was starting a label called eleven-eleven. Her first act was twelve-year-old Greyson Chance, a sensation on YouTube with his piano version of Lady Gaga's "Paparazzi."

That same year, she achieved a spot on the list of the 20 Richest Women in Entertainment, which requires a minimum net worth of $45 million. She was included in *Forbes'* Top 5 Most Influential Women in Media list and was voted Best Daytime Talk-Show Host by Parade.com. The annual Harris Poll voted her Favorite TV Personality over world-renowned hosts like Oprah Winfrey and Jay Leno. She was honored with Television Week's Syndication Personality of the Year and voted to the top of Oxygen's 50 Funniest Women Alive special, joining comedy legends such as Carol Burnett and Lily Tomlin. She has also been included in *Time's* 100 Most Influential People. In 2012, she

Ellen is one of the most famous entertainers in the world today.
She was awarded her own star on the well-known Hollywood
Walk of Fame in 2012.

received her very own star on Hollywood's Walk of Fame. That same year, JCPenney, the company that had once refused to run ads on her show, asked her to become their advertising spokesperson.

True Success

Ellen has shot far past any of her earlier dreams of success. Despite her fame and fortune, though, she has learned to define success differently from what she once did. She told the graduates at Tulane, "My idea of success is different today. For me the most important thing in your life is to live your life with integrity, and not to give in to peer pressure, to try to be something that you're not."

Ellen doesn't think she could have reached this point without the hard times that came with her public coming out. "It was so important for me to lose everything," she said, "because I found what the most important thing is—to be true to yourself. Ultimately, that's what's gotten me to this place. I don't live in fear. I'm free. I have no secrets. And I know I'll always be okay, because no matter what, I know who I am."

Ellen has helped others to know who they are too. She receives thousands of letters from LGBT people all over the world. People she's never met feel a connection to her because she lives her life so openly and honestly. She tells them, "Live your life as an honest and compassionate person, to contribute in some way. . . . Follow your passion. Stay true to yourself. And never follow someone else's path."

LGBT
Historical Timeline

In the twenty-first century, the world has become more and more tolerant of homosexuality. But prejudice and discrimination are still all too common.

2007: On August 9, the cable network Logo hosts a presidential debate that focuses around gay issues. While all of the candidates, both Republican and Democrat, are invited to participate, the Democrat candidates are the only ones who come. Participants are Hillary Clinton, John Edwards, and Barack Obama. The same year, researchers estimate that nearly 255,000 men who have engaged in homosexual sex are living with HIV/AIDS, while about 5,400 have died. The first gay pride parade is held in a Muslim country in Istanbul, Turkey.

2009: Iceland elects Jóhanna Sigurðardóttir as prime minister; she is the world's first openly gay leader of a national government.

2010: The National Gay and Lesbian Task Force finds that 45 percent of gay males and 20 percent of lesbians surveyed have experienced verbal bullying and or physical violence during high school as a result of their sexual orientation. In a survey of lesbians and gay men in

Pennsylvania, 33 percent of gay men and 34 percent of lesbians report suffering physical violence at the hands of a family member as a result of their sexual orientation. In a study of 484 students at six community colleges, 18 percent of the men interviewed admit that they had committed physical violence or threats against men and/or women they perceived to be gay or lesbian.

2011: The U.S. military's Don't-Ask-Don't-Tell policy comes to an end, and gays are openly allowed in the American armed forces.

2013: Homosexuality is no longer against the law in the nation of Benin—but India passes laws that once again make homosexual acts punishable crimes. President Barack Obama talks about gay rights in his inaugural address, and "Same Love," a hit single from Macklemore and Ryan Lewis, becomes the first top-40 song in the United States to celebrate same-sex marriage.

Here are some words and phrases you'll need to understand:

Animal rights is the idea that nonhuman animals have many of the same rights as humans, especially the right to not suffer pain. Because of her belief in animal rights, Ellen does not eat meat.

Prejudice has to do with opinions that aren't based on actual knowledge or experience. If you were prejudiced against green eggs and ham, for example, you would refuse to try them simply because you *thought* they would taste bad, even though you really had no idea. Prejudice could also cause you to judge others based on those people being different from you in some way, even though you really don't know those people.

Chapter Four

Making a Difference

Ellen follows her own path—and that path continues to change others' lives.

The Ellen DeGeneres Show has raised more than $50 million to support many different charities. After Hurricane Katrina devastated the city of New Orleans, the show brought in more than $10 million to help the residents of the city. Ellen also uses her show to bring attention to causes such as global warming, breast cancer, and animal rights. She has served as a spokesperson for General Mills' breast cancer awareness project, Pink for the Cure, and hosted special fundraising episodes of her show to mark Breast Cancer Awareness Month.

Love and Marriage

In 2004, Ellen fell in love with Australian actress Portia de Rossi, who had risen to fame with television roles on *Ally McBeal* and

Ellen has been with actress Portia de Rossi for years. The two have become one of the most famous gay couples in Hollywood.

Same-Sex Marriage in California

Same-sex marriages were legal in the state of California for only a short period during 2008—and then the voters of California made them illegal again with the passage of a law called Proposition 8. Anyone who had gotten married during the time that it was legal—including Ellen and Portia—were still considered to be legally married, but they did not have the full rights of same-sex married couples.

Ellen wrote a letter to the Supreme Court, asking that the court overturn Proposition 8. In it, she said, "Even though Portia and I got married in the short period of time when it was legal in California, there are 1,138 federal rights for married couples that we don't have, including some that protect married people from losing their homes, or their savings or custody of their children. The truth is, Portia and I aren't as different from you as you might think. We're just trying to find happiness in the bodies and minds we were given, like everyone else. I hope the Supreme Court will do the right thing, and let everyone enjoy the same rights. . . . It is time."

On June 28, 2013, the U.S. Supreme Court overturned Proposition 8, and same-sex marriages were once again legal in California.

Arrested Development. In 2008, in the state of California where Ellen and Portia lived, the couple had a wonderful opportunity.

"This is very exciting, I gotta say," Ellen said on her show. "Yesterday, if you haven't heard, the California Supreme Court overturned a ban on gay marriage."

Ellen and Portia's example gave other couples the courage to take the same big step.

The audience cheered, and then she continued, "So I would like to say, for the first time, I am announcing I am getting married."

The audience, which included Portia, went crazy. Ellen's eyes filled with tears. "If I'm this emotional now just saying it, I can't imagine how that's gonna be," she laughed. "It's something that of course we've wanted to do, and we wanted it to be legal, and we're just very excited."

Ellen and Portia were married in a small ceremony with only nineteen guests, including the couple's mothers. They live together today in Beverly Hills, with three dogs and four cats.

The impact of their marriage has been enormous. Just like when Ellen came out on primetime TV, she had now brought the issue of same-sex marriage out into the open. Millions of people saw the couple's wedding video when Ellen aired it on her show and then later made it available online. Once again Ellen was using her celebrity status to open up people's minds and fight prejudice.

True to Herself

Ellen has achieved enormous success, beyond her wildest dreams, but she's not planning on taking it easy anytime soon. She continues to want to make a difference in the world. She told Oprah, "I constantly challenge myself. . . . When something goes wrong, instead of running away from it, I look at it and go, 'What's my part in it, what's my responsibility?'"

In 2010, when several young adults committed suicide after they were bullied for being gay, Ellen spoke out. She said, "Being a teenager and figuring out who you are is hard enough

Ellen and Portia were married in a small ceremony among friends after laws changed to allow same-sex marriage in California.

without someone attacking you. . . . I want anyone out there who feels different and alone to know I know how you feel. . . . Things will get easier. People's minds will change. You should be alive to see it."

In one of her books, Ellen offers this advice to us all: "Find out who you are and figure out what you believe in. Even if it's different from what your neighbors believe in and different from what your parents believe in. Stay true to yourself. Have your own opinion. Don't worry about what people say about you or think about you. Let the naysayers nay. They will eventually grow tired of naying."

Ellen knows that although she has millions of fans, not everyone approves of her or her lifestyle. "I can't really do anything about that," she says. "I wish I could make people see there is nothing wrong with being who you are. . . . I used to want people to like me and I still want them to like me, but I know I have no control over it. . . . I live my life in a kind way. I go to sleep at night and know I've done the best I can. That's all I can do."

Now that Ellen has learned to stand up and be counted, she doesn't plan to ever stop.

Same-Sex Marriage Timeline

You'll notice a few different terms used in this timeline. Same-sex partnerships, domestic partnerships, and civil unions give some rights to couples, but they are not the same as marriage, which guarantees couples the most legal privileges. Most governments start out by granting a lower level of rights to same-sex couples. That's usually the first step—and then it may take years before same-sex marriages become legal in that same country or state. This timeline reveals how public opinion changes over time—and how public opinion can then change government policies.

1979: The Netherlands becomes the first country in the world where same-sex couples can apply for limited legal rights.

1989: Denmark becomes the first country in the world to legally recognize same-sex unions.

1993: Norway becomes the second country in the world to provide legal recognition for same-sex couples.

1994: Sweden approves legal recognition of same-sex partnerships.

1996: Iceland legalizes registered same-sex partnerships. Meanwhile, in the United States, the Defense of Marriage Act becomes law, banning the federal government from recognizing same-sex unions.

1998: Hawaii and Alaska become the first U.S. states to pass constitutional amendments against same-sex marriage. Other U.S. states follow suit and passed similar amendments in the following years. Meanwhile, Belgium legally recognizes registered same-sex partnerships.

2000: The state of California signs a domestic partnerships bill into law that provides limited rights for same-sex couples, and the state of Vermont gives full marriage rights to same-sex couples. France redefines a legal form of partnership as "the stable union between two adults regardless of their gender." Germany approves a bill to legalize Life Partnerships. The Netherlands signs into law the first same-sex marriage bill in the world.

2001: Belgium becomes the second country in the world to legalize civil marriage for same-sex couples. The Canadian province of Ontario legalizes same-sex marriages.

2004: Several U.S. states issue marriage licenses to same-sex couples. Same-sex marriage becomes legal in Massachusetts, while Connecticut, New Hampshire and New Jersey legalize same-sex civil unions, and Washington State and Oregon sign domestic partnerships into law.

The UK parliament legalizes civil partnerships for same-sex couples, and South Africa rules that the common law concept of marriage must be extended to include same-sex couples. Other nations take similar actions, including Israel, New Zealand, Andorra, Switzerland, Slovenia, Spain, Canada, the Czech Republic, and Uruguay.

2008: Connecticut, Iowa, Vermont, the District of Columbia, Maine, and California legalize same-sex marriages (though voters take back the California and Maine decisions later), while Maryland legalizes domestic partnerships. Wisconsin signs into law the recognition of registered same-sex partnerships. Meanwhile, some form of same-sex civil partnerships become legal in Australia, Norway, Ecuador, Nepal, Colombia, Sweden, Hungary, Austria, and Mexico. The first legal same-sex marriage takes place in Greece.

2010: Same-sex marriages become legal in Portugal, Iceland, and Argentina.

2011: The U.S. states of Illinois, Delaware, Rhode Island, and Hawaii sign civil unions bills into law. New York State legalizes same-sex marriages. Brazil and Australia legalize civil unions

2012: Washington, Maine, and Maryland make same-sex marriages legal, as do the nations of Denmark and Mexico.

2013: Colorado signs a civil unions bill into law, and Rhode Island, Minnesota, New Mexico, Hawaii, and

Delaware sign same-sex marriage bills into law, and same-sex marriage becomes legal in California again. Uruguay, Brazil, France, England, Wales, Australia, and New Zealand legalize same-sex marriages—but Croatia passes a constitutional amendment banning same-sex marriage and defining marriage as strictly a union between a man and woman. The U.S. District Court for Utah finds the state's ban on same-sex marriage unconstitutional.

2014: The U.S. District Court for Oklahoma finds the state's ban on same-sex marriage unconstitutional, while same-sex marriage becomes legal in New Jersey.

Find Out More

In Books

Beige, Kathy. *Queer: The Ultimate LGBT Guide for Teens*. San Francisco, Calif.: Zest, 2011.

DeGeneres, Betty. *Love, Ellen: A Mother/Daughter Journey*. New York: It Books, 2000.

DeGeneres, Ellen. *The Funny Thing Is. . . .* New York: Simon & Schuster, 2004.

——. *My Point . . . And I Do Have One*. New York: Bantam, 2007.

——. *Seriously . . . I'm Kidding (reprint edition)*. New York: Grand Central Publishing, 2012.

Savage, Dan and Terry Miller (editors). *It Gets Better: Coming Out, Overcoming Bullying, and Creating a Life Worth Living*. New York: Plume, 2012.

Online

Coming Out as an LGBT Teen
teens.webmd.com/features/coming-out-as-lgbt-teen

The Ellen DeGeneres Show
www.ellentv.com

Ellen DeGeneres Facebook Page
www.facebook.com/ellentv

Empty Closets
emptyclosets.com

Human Rights Campaign Coming Out Center
www.hrc.org/campaigns/coming-out-center

The Trevor Project
www.thetrevorproject.org

Index

About the Author

Rae Simons has written many books for young adults and children. She lives with her family in New York State.

Picture Credits

Dreamstime.com:
8: Zsolt Ercsei
16: Juan Moyano
34: Featureflash
36: Carrienelson1
38: Pindiyath100
40: Sbukley
42: Sbukley

44: Featureflash
50: Sbukley
52: Howesjwe
54: Featureflash

12: *Time* Magazine
24: Danlev / Dan Leveille
26: Tulane Public Relations

CPSIA information can be obtained
at www.ICGtesting.com
Printed in the USA
LVOW05*0105150916

504683LV00018B/354/P